ALONG THE SHORE

DISCOVERING SEAGULLS

Lorijo Metz

PowerKiDS press™

New York

To Henry and Missy . . . always scavenging, always begging, always finding new ways to get more food

Published in 2012 by The Rosen Publishing Group, Inc.
29 East 21st Street, New York, NY 10010

First Edition

Editor: Amelie von Zumbusch
Book Design: Kate Laczynski

Photo Credits: Cover Deborah Harrison/Getty Images; pp. 4–5, 6, 7, 8, 9 (top, bottom), 14–15, 16, 17 (top), 18, 19 (top), 21 Shutterstock.com; pp. 10, 11 (top), 12 iStockphoto/Thinkstock; p. 11 (bottom) © www.iStockphoto.com/Reagan Lewis Payseur; p. 13 Chris Warde-Jones/Bloomberg/Getty Images; p. 17 (bottom) Jupiterimages/Photos.com/Thinkstock; p. 20 Hemera/Thinkstock; p. 22 Brand X Pictures/Thinkstock.

Library of Congress Cataloging-in-Publication Data

Metz, Lorijo.
 Discovering seagulls / by Lorijo Metz. — 1st ed.
     p. cm. — (Along the shore)
 Includes index.
 ISBN 978-1-4488-4995-6 (library binding)
 1. Gulls—Juvenile literature. I. Title.
 QL696.C46M48 2012
 598.3'38—dc22

                              2011000154

Manufactured in the United States of America

CPSIA Compliance Information: Batch #WS11PK: For Further Information contact Rosen Publishing, New York, New York at 1-800-237-9932

CONTENTS

SPOTTING SEAGULLS

If you take a walk along a crowded beach, chances are good that you will see seagulls. Seagulls often gather around people. This is because they love our food!

Over the years, seagulls have **adapted**, or gotten used, to living near people. The birds know that where people gather, food is near. Seagulls have been known

These seagulls are sitting on rocks along the shore. Seagulls are a common sight along the shore.

to steal food from people. They also eat food that people have thrown away. In fact, you can sometimes see them picking food out of the trash!

Seagulls are sometimes known as gulls. In fact, not all gulls live by the sea. Some are found far inland.

SEAGULL FACT

Seagulls are found along almost every coast in the world except for some central Pacific islands and parts of Southeast Asia.

WHAT DO SEAGULLS LOOK LIKE?

Seagull feathers tend to be gray, black, and white. Seagulls have long wings and are skilled fliers. They often just catch the wind and float on it.

There are several **species**, or types, of gulls. Depending on its species, a gull's **wingspan** can

This is a silver gull. These seagulls are common in Australia and New Zealand. Adult silver gulls have red beaks, feet, and legs.

measure between 24 and 63 inches (61–160 cm) from the tip of one wing to the tip of the other.

Like many birds that live near water, seagulls have **webbed** feet. Folds of skin, called webbing, connect three long toes in front and one short toe in back. The gulls' paddlelike feet are perfect for swimming.

DIFFERENT TYPES OF SEAGULLS

There are more than 40 species of gulls in the world. More than 20 of these live in North America. Herring gulls are one of the most common gulls. While most live by the ocean, many have adapted to living in cities and towns along the shore. Herring gulls are know for their laughing call.

Great black-backed gulls can grow to be 31 inches (79 cm) long, from head to tail. These seagulls live in eastern North America.

These are laughing gulls. Laughing gulls live in North America and South America. Their call sounds like someone laughing loudly.

Great black-backed gulls are the largest species of seagull. They are so large that they can swallow small wild ducks whole! Little gulls are the smallest seagulls. They live along coasts and around lakes. They are the only gulls to have babies in both the Caribbean Sea and the North Atlantic Ocean.

Bonaparte's gulls live in North America. They spend the summer in Alaska and northern Canada. They are the only gulls that nest in trees.

9

WHAT DO SEAGULLS EAT?

Seagulls eat nearly everything! They are **opportunistic feeders**. This means they tend to eat whatever food happens to be nearest. Near the ocean, they eat fish, snails, clams, and other shellfish. Western gulls dine on squid and jellyfish. They will even eat dead seals and sea lions! Ross's gulls spend the summer eating mostly insects, such as beetles and flies.

SEAGULL FACT

Seagulls drink freshwater, found in lakes and rivers, and salt water, found in oceans. Most animals cannot drink salt water. Gulls have a special way of getting rid of the salt from their bodies, though.

This gull is picking at a dead fish on a beach. Seagulls often eat things that wash up on beaches.

This seagull is eating a starfish. Seagulls sometimes pick starfish out of tide pools. Tide pools are formed by the tide washing up over rocky beaches.

Away from the water, seagulls gather wherever people throw away food. Have you ever wondered where your trash goes? Most trash is buried in **landfills**. Landfills are one of seagulls' favorite places to find food.

Seagulls often steal food. This seagull is stealing a fish from a fishing boat.

NATURE'S SCAVENGERS

Seagulls are natural **scavengers**. They search for food wherever they can. Seagulls often catch small animals, such as crabs, along the shore. Gulls steal food from other seagulls, too. Some seagulls even eat seagull eggs and chicks.

This fishing boat is being followed by dozens of seagulls. Seagulls can seem like pests to people who work on fishing boats.

These seagulls are visiting a landfill outside of Rome, Italy, to look for food. Seagulls are common at landfills.

Seagulls like to follow boats, waiting for people to toss food over the side. When fishermen are not looking, seagulls may take fish from their nets. They pluck insects out of the air and catch fish swimming in the water. To eat shellfish, such as clams, seagulls drop them from up high. When the shellfish hit the ground, their shells break open. The gulls can then eat their soft insides.

MIGRATION AND COMMUNICATION

Most seagulls stay in the same place all year long. Seagulls from colder parts of the world **migrate**, or fly south in the winter, though. Laughing gulls that spend the summer in the northeastern United States spend the winter in Florida, Central America, or South America. Seagulls sometimes wander off as they migrate. They can end up far from their normal

The seagulls that do migrate sometimes travel in big flocks. Some of these flocks have tens of thousands of birds.

nesting grounds. This can lead to seagulls of different species **breeding**, or producing chicks, together.

Seagulls **communicate**, or talk, using movements and sounds. A long trumpetlike call means a herring gull is going to stand fast, or refuse to move. When herring gulls are angry, they try to make themselves look bigger.

MATING AND NESTING

Male and female seagulls **mate**, or come together to build nests and lay eggs. Most seagulls mate in the spring. Mated seagulls will stay together for years. In the winter, mates sometimes join different **flocks**, or groups. They generally still find each other again in the spring, though. Mates often return to the same place to nest.

These laughing gulls are courting. Courting is the way that a bird picks another bird for a mate.

This seagull is sitting on its nest overlooking the ocean. As you can see, the nest is made of small sticks and grass.

Most seagulls build their nests in the ground or on the side of cliffs. The nests are far away from enemies, such as people. Nests are made of seaweed, sticks, and other plants. Seagulls that have adapted to living in cities, such as herring gulls and black-headed gulls, may build their nests on rooftops.

Some kinds of seagulls form nesting colonies. These are places where lots of birds build their nests close together.

GROWING UP AS A SEAGULL

Seagulls mate once a year. Females lay two to four eggs at a time. Parents take turns sitting on the eggs to keep them warm. Most chicks hatch, or break free of their shells, after 20 to 30 days. Chicks remain in their parents' nest for about six months. Their parents feed them by chewing the

SEAGULL FACT

To stay warm while they rest, seagulls stand on one leg. They lose heat most quickly through their legs. Pulling one leg up against its body helps a gull lose less heat.

This adult seagull is keeping watch while its chick snuggles up underneath its wing.

Yellow-legged gulls, such as this chick, are born along the shores of the Mediterranean Sea. When they get older, they may visit places inland in Africa, Asia, and Europe.

food first, swallowing it, then bringing it back up to give to the chicks.

Young seagulls are often born with brown or gray feathers. They will **molt**, or lose their feathers, each year until they get their adult feathers. For larger species, this can take up to four years.

This is a juvenile yellow-legged gull. In between being chicks and adults, gulls are juveniles. Juveniles have different coloring than either chicks or adults.

SEAGULLS AND PEOPLE

Seagulls help keep our beaches clean by eating dead fish along the shore. Fishermen sometimes follow herring gulls to good fishing spots.

In 1995, Utah made the California gull its state bird. These gulls are found both along the Pacific coast and farther inland. Stories tell of California gulls that saved Utah's Mormon settlers by eating

Seagulls are a common sight in parks, such as this one along the coast of the Pacific Ocean.

grasshoppers that were destroying their crops in 1848.

The friendship between seagulls and people is not simple, though. More and more seagulls have started living in cities and towns. In cities, seagulls can be a danger to low-flying airplanes. Seagull droppings and nests can ruin roofs, too.

21

HISTORY AND BEYOND

Years ago, people used seagull feathers to make hats. Some people ate seagull eggs and even chicks. Today, few people would consider eating a seagull.

Over the years, some seagull species have been in danger of dying out. Each time, though, their numbers have come back. Laws, such as

Whether they are flying along a beautiful beach or heading toward an ugly landfill, seagulls are very graceful in the air.

the 2000 New Jersey Conservation of Wildlife Law, have helped seagulls. Seagulls survive mainly because they adapt. Whether nesting on rooftops or sharing the beaches with us, seagulls have found ways to live alongside people.

adapted (uh-DAPT-ed) Changed to fit new conditions.

breeding (BREED-ing) Having babies together.

communicate (kuh-MYOO-nih-kayt) To share facts or feelings.

flocks (FLOKS) Groups of birds.

landfills (LAND-filz) Places where waste is buried between layers of earth.

mate (MAYT) To come together to make babies.

migrate (MY-grayt) To move from one place to another.

molt (MOHLT) To shed hair, feathers, shell, horns, or skin.

opportunistic feeders (o-pur-too-NIS-tik FEE-derz) Animals that eat whatever they can find.

scavengers (SKA-ven-jurz) Animals that eat dead things.

species (SPEE-sheez) One kind of living thing. All people are one species.

webbed (WEBD) Having skin between the toes, as ducks, frogs, and other animals that swim do.

wingspan (WING-span) The distance from wing tip to wing tip when a bird's wings are stretched out.

INDEX

WEB SITES

Due to the changing nature of Internet links, PowerKids Press has developed an online list of Web sites related to the subject of this book. This site is updated regularly. Please use this link to access the list:

www.powerkidslinks.com/alsh/seagulls/